Maxwell

by Murray Ogilvie

79 Main Street, Newtongrange,
Midlothian EH22 4NA
Tel: 0131 344 0414
E-mail: info@lang-syne.co.uk
www.langsyneshop.co.uk

Design by Dorothy Meikle
Printed by Printwell Ltd
© Lang Syne Publishers Ltd 2025

All rights reserved. No part of this publication may be reproduced, stored or introduced into a retrieval system, or transmitted in any form or by any means (electronic, mechanical, photocopying, recording or otherwise) without the prior written permission of Lang Syne Publishers Ltd.

ISBN 978-1-85217-320-3

Maxwell

SEPT NAMES:

- Adair
- Blackstock
- Dinwiddie
- Dinwoddie
- Edgar
- Herries
- Kirk
- Kirkland
- Latimer
- Latimore
- Mackittrick
- Maxton
- Mescall
- Monreith
- Moss
- Nithdale
- Paulk
- Peacock
- Pollock
- Pollok
- Polk
- Sturgeon
- Wardlaw

Maxwell

MOTTO:
Reviresco
("I flourish again").

CREST:
A stag standing in front
of a holly bush.

TERRITORY:
The Borders.

Chapter one:

The origins of the clan system

by Rennie McOwan

The original Scottish clans of the Highlands and the great families of the Lowlands and Borders were gatherings of families, relatives, allies and neighbours for mutual protection against rivals or invaders.

Scotland experienced invasion from the Vikings, the Romans and English armies from the south. The Norman invasion of what is now England also had an influence on land-holding in Scotland. Some of these invaders stayed on and in time became 'Scottish'.

The word clan derives from the Gaelic language term 'clann', meaning children, and it was first used many centuries ago as communities were formed around tribal lands in glens and mountain fastnesses.

The format of clans changed over the centuries, but at its best the chief and his family held the land on behalf of all, like trustees, and the ordinary clansmen and women believed they had a blood relationship with the founder of their clan.

There were two way duties and obligations. An inadequate chief could be deposed and replaced by someone of greater ability.

Clan people had an immense pride in race. Their relationship with the chief was like adult children to a father and they had a real dignity.

The concept of clanship is very old and a more feudal notion of authority gradually crept in.

Pictland, for instance, was divided into seven principalities ruled by feudal leaders who were the strongest and most charismatic leaders of their particular groups.

By the sixth century the 'British' kingdoms of Strathclyde, Lothian and Celtic Dalriada (Argyll) had emerged and Scotland, as one nation, began to take shape in the time of King Kenneth MacAlpin.

Some chiefs claimed descent from

ancient kings which may not have been accurate in every case.

By the twelfth and thirteenth centuries the clans and families were more strongly brought under the central control of Scottish monarchs.

Lands were awarded and administered more and more under royal favour, yet the power of the area clan chiefs was still very great.

The long wars to ensure Scotland's independence against the expansionist ideas of English monarchs extended the influence of some clans and reduced the lands of others.

Those who supported Scotland's greatest king, Robert the Bruce, were awarded the territories of the families who had opposed his claim to the Scottish throne.

In the Scottish Borders country – the notorious Debatable Lands – the great families built up a ferocious reputation for providing warlike men accustomed to raiding into England and occasionally fighting one another.

Chiefs had the power to dispense justice and to confiscate lands and clan warfare produced a society where martial virtues – courage, hardiness, tenacity – were greatly admired.

Gradually the relationship between the clans and the Crown became strained as Scottish monarchs became more orientated to life in the Lowlands and, on occasion, towards England.

The Highland clans spoke a different language, Gaelic, whereas the language of Lowland Scotland and the court was Scots and in more modern times, English.

Highlanders dressed differently, had different customs, and their wild mountain land sometimes seemed almost foreign to people living in the Lowlands.

It must be emphasised that Gaelic culture was very rich and story-telling, poetry, piping, the clarsach (harp) and other music all flourished and were greatly respected.

Highland culture was different from other parts of Scotland but it was not inferior or less sophisticated.

Central Government, whether in London or Edinburgh, sometimes saw the Gaelic clans as

"The spirit of the clan means much to thousands of people"

a challenge to their authority and some sent expeditions into the Highlands and west to crush the power of the Lords of the Isles.

Nevertheless, when the eighteenth century Jacobite Risings came along the cause of the Stuarts was mainly supported by Highland clans.

The word Jacobite comes from the Latin for James – Jacobus. The Jacobites wanted to restore the exiled Stuarts to the throne of Britain.

The monarchies of Scotland and England became one in 1603 when King James VI of Scotland (1st of England) gained the English throne after Queen Elizabeth died.

The Union of Parliaments of Scotland and England, the Treaty of Union, took place in 1707.

Some Highland clans, of course, and Lowland families opposed the Jacobites and supported the incoming Hanoverians.

After the Jacobite cause finally went down at Culloden in 1746 a kind of ethnic cleansing took place. The power of the chiefs was curtailed. Tartan and the pipes were banned in law.

Many emigrated, some because they

wanted to, some because they were evicted by force. In addition, many Highlanders left for the cities of the south to seek work.

Many of the clan lands became home to sheep and deer shooting estates.

But the warlike traditions of the clans and the great Lowland and Border families lived on, with their descendants fighting bravely for freedom in two world wars.

Remember the men from whence you came, says the Gaelic proverb, and to that could be added the role of many heroic women.

The spirit of the clan, of having roots, whether Highland or Lowland, means much to thousands of people.

Clan warfare produced a society where courage and tenacity were greatly admired

Chapter two:

From Maccus...

The Maxwells are an old and respected Borders clan, who can trace their origin back to the 12th century. They appear to have become a prominent and wealthy family very quickly and continued to occupy the higher echelons of Scottish life for many centuries.

They became Wardens of the West Marches, Stewards of Kirkcudbright and Annandale, ambassadors to England, and Provosts of Edinburgh. In addition there were peerages – Baron Maxwell, Baron Herries, Baron Eskdale, Baron Carlyle, Earl of Morton and Earl of Nithsdale.

The clan took its name from Maccus, a Saxon noble, who had fled England at the time of the Norman Conquest. During his stay in Scotland King David ascended to the throne. He had been brought up in England and had married the great niece of William the Conqueror. David was a devotee of Anglo-Norman culture and was determined to see it spread in Scotland. To that extent he rewarded Anglo-Normans who settled north of the border. Maccus was granted lands on the banks of the Tweed, near Kelso. He later gave his name to a salmon pool on the river, which became known as Maccuswell. The second part of the name came from "wael", the old English word for pool. The adjacent lands got the name, and the descendants of Maccus became known as, "de" Maccuswael. It is not difficult to envisage the name evolving from de Maccuswael to Maxwell!

Maccus's oldest son was Herbert of Maccuswell, who became the Sheriff of Teviotdale. He gifted the family's church to Kelso Abbey sometime before his death in 1143. It was customary in those days to make such gifts to abbots who, in turn, would pray for the souls of their benefactors.

The Maxwells' marriages to other great Scottish families – Crichton, Douglas, Hamilton, Herries, Seton and the Stewart brought them greater power and riches.

One example of how their influence was consolidated through marriage can be traced via the family's history through 100 or so years from the 16th to the 17th centuries.

John Maxwell, the younger brother of Robert the sixth Lord Maxwell, married Agnes Herries. She was the eldest daughter and sole heiress of William, the third Lord Herries. Mr Maxwell became the fourth Lord Herries of Terregles. He died in 1582.

In 1667, Robert the eleventh Lord Maxwell and by now the second earl of Nithsdale died without marrying. His title went to his relative, John Maxwell, who just happened to be a direct descendant of the fourth Lord Herries. So John Maxwell became twelfth Lord Maxwell, seventh Lord Herries and third earl of Nithsdale, thus uniting two great landowning families in one man.

Chapter three:

Maxwell's House

Although the Maxwells hail from Kelso, they soon spread their influential wings right across southern and western Scotland and became among the greatest property-owning families in Scottish history. Over the years they built many castles and stately homes.

Caerlaverock Castle, between Annan and Dumfries, became a symbol of Maxwell prestige. It was built by Maccus's grandson, Sir John de Maccuswell, who became Sheriff of Roxburgh and Teviotdale and later, around the year 1230 was made royal Chamberlain. It was involved in one of the most famous battles in Scottish history. During the first war of Scottish independence against the English it was besieged by King Edward's army. The year was 1300 and Sir John's grandson, Sir Herbert Maxwell lived at Caerlaverock. He was a Scottish patriot and was determined to resist Edward's attempts to subdue the whole of Scotland. The English monarch brought an army of thousands which included 87 of the most illustrious English barons along with knights from Bretagne and Lorraine. Despite this overwhelming force the castle, well-prepared and designed to withstand a lengthy siege, refused to capitulate. The Maxwells hit their attackers with everything they could, causing massive losses. But eventually they were forced to surrender. It was only then it was discovered that the pride of the English army had been kept at bay by just 60 men. Caerlaverock was eventually given back to the Maxwells and Sir Herbert's son, Sir Eustace became the owner. He became a supporter of John Baliol as king of Scotland. However, with typical Maxwell pragmatism he switched sides and joined Robert Bruce. In the ensuing war Caerlaverock Castle was again under siege. But it had been re-fortified, ironically thanks to cash provided by the English who supported Baliol, and this time it managed to hold out. However, the Bruce was worried that such an impregnable strategic fortress could fall into the wrong hands and persuaded Sir Eustace to dismantle it. Sir Eustace was encouraged by a great financial reward as well as his loyalty.

Maxwell's Castle in nearby Dumfries was built in the fifteenth century and contained barracks which could house 200 men. It was bought by the people of Dumfries who pulled it

Robert The Bruce

down in 1720 and built a church on the site. In 1866 it too was demolished and Greyfriars Church was built.

Hoddom Castle, just east of Dumfries, is now a popular caravan park. It was built by Sir John Maxwell of Terregles in the 16th century as part of a defensive line across the border and was empty more often than not. It was sold in 1626 by Sir John's grandson, William, Lord Herries and after it changed hands several more times it was requisitioned during WWII and was occupied by allied servicemen. In the 1950s, having fallen into disrepair much of it was demolished. Today all that remains are remnants of a 16th and 17th century towerhouse.

The fifteenth century **Terregles Castle**, a couple of miles northwest of Dumfries, was the seat of Lord Herries. It passed to the Maxwells in around 1540 when Agnes Herries married Sir John Maxwell. Mary, Queen of Scots spent several days there in 1568 recovering after losing the Battle of Langside before she fled into England. It was from here that the fifth Earl of Nithsdale rode out to join the rebellion of 1715. After he was captured at Preston, Lady Nithsdale buried the family papers and valuables in the grounds. It was demolished in the 1800s.

Newark Castle was built in the fifteenth century by George Maxwell, the second son of Sir William Maxwell of Calderwood. It stood on the banks of the Clyde with views to Dumbarton. King James IV stayed there in 1495. George Maxwell of Newark and Tealing (1678-1744) spent a fortune on his horses and was forced to sell Newark in 1705.

In 1674 the Maxwell sold to the city of Glasgow 18 acres of land to the west of the castle, which was used to construct a new port for Glasgow. It became the modern Port Glasgow and its mass of shipyards hid the castle from public view for nearly 100 years. When the ship building industry collapsed in the second half of the 20th century and with it the great structures which had dominated the countryside, a medieval castle, which is now in the care of Historic Scotland, appeared.

Calderwood Castle was the home of the Maxwells of Calderwood from the end of the 14th century until it was sold in 1904. In stood in Calderglen, which is now a public park in East Kilbride. Other land owned by the family included the area now occupied by Glasgow Airport and the barony of Dargavel, which became the Bishopton munitions works.

Mearns Castle was built in 1449 just south of Glasgow. The area had been in Maxwell possession since the early thirteenth century. The lords Maxwell never lived there, preferring the south-west of Scotland. Today only a single tower remains. It can be seen in the affluent Glasgow suburb of Newton Mearns, where the local parish church has been attached to its northern facade, with the old castle forming the church steeple.

Haggs Castle was part of the Nether Pollok barony in Renfrewshire, although it has since been swallowed up by the city of Glasgow. A carved stone over the entrance confirms it was built by Sir John Maxwell of Pollok and his wife

Margaret Cunningham in 1585. Haggs is now the oldest secular building in domestic use in Glasgow. It was used to house Sir John's growing extended family who were based at nearby Nether Pollok. From the 1680s it was a dower house, for the ladies of the family. It had large gardens and orchards but was never endowed with farm lands of its own. In the 18th century old Nether Pollok Castle was replaced by the comfortable new Robert Adam designed Pollok House and the Ladies moved there, abandoning Haggs. By the 1860s, Sir John Maxwell of Pollok began selling bits of his estates to the city of Glasgow who built new houses on them. Sir John used the money to restore the old castle and it became the house and offices for the Estate Factor. It was requisitioned by the army during WWII and in the late 1940s the Maxwell Trustees converted it into flats. In 1972 it was bought by Glasgow Corporation, and converted for use as a children's museum. In 1997 it was sold again and is now a private residence. Up until the end of the 19th century it was surrounded by open countryside. Today it is part of of

Pollokshields, one of Scotland's wealthiest neighbourhoods where mansions change hands for more than £1 million. The area is full of names commemorating the Maxwells' influence. Haggs Castle is an exclusive golf club. Maxwell Park is a public area and nearby roads are named Maxwell, Nithsdale, Herries, Terregles, Springkell, and Haggs. Nearby is the large Pollok Park, which houses Pollok House and the Nether Pollok playing fields. It splits the neighborhoods of Pollok and Pollokshaws. The whole area was part of the Pollok Estate which had been owned by the Maxwell family since the mid-13th century. In its midst is Pollok House, an 18th century mansion, filled with Spanish art, antique furniture, silverware, ceramics and an impressive library. Most of the paintings were collected by Sir William Stirling Maxwell (1818-1878). In 1966 Pollok House was gifted by Mrs Anne Maxwell Macdonald to the City of Glasgow, along with its art collection and 361 acres of surrounding parkland which contain the world-famous Burrell Collection.

Chapter four:

The Great Escape

One of the most celebrated incidents in the clan's history concerns the daring escape from the Tower of London by William Maxwell, who was 14th Lord Maxwell, 9th Lord Herries and 3rd Earl of Nithsdale. He was born in 1676 and was a Roman Catholic who had joined the Jacobite cause to bring back the exiled House of Stuart to the Scottish and English thrones. In 1715 he was captured after the Jacobites were routed at the Battle of Preston. He was sent to the Tower of London and sentenced to death.

However, on the eve of his execution he escaped thanks to the sheer brilliance and daring of his wife, Winifred.

When she arrived in London she immediately set about garnering support for her husband's release. When she found out that there was little or no chance of a pardon she decided to put her carefully conceived plan into action. The countess confided in her lady in waiting because she required her help. On February 22, 1716, a petition supporting her husband's release was to be debated in the House of Lords. The Lords agreed that the king had the power to intercede and grant a pardon and the countess viewed that as only a partial victory and realised more drastic action was required if she were to save her beloved husband's life. She went to the Tower and told the guards that the Lords had voted in favour of an amnesty and then gave them some money to buy drinks to toast her success. This was two days before the execution.

The following night, on the eve of the execution, she urged Mrs Mills, with whom she'd been lodging and Mrs Morgan, a friend of a friend, to assist her in the plot. Both readily agreed. The plan called for Mrs Morgan, who was tall and slender, to smuggle a change of clothes for Mrs Mills into the Earl's cell. Mrs Mills, who was pregnant and therefore almost the same shape as the Earl, would leave her clothes behind for him and exit the Tower wearing the clothes which had been smuggled in.

On arrival the countess and Mrs Morgan

entered the cell. The countess was allowed only one other visitor with her at a time. She quickly removed the extra set of clothes and left. Next Mrs Mills was invited in. The brilliant countess had taken the precaution of stocking up on paint. Mrs Mills's eyebrows were sandy coloured while the Earl's were dark and she intended to paint his to match her lighter shade. In addition the countess had an artificial head dress which matched the colour of Mrs Mills's hair. Finally she painted her husband's face white and added rouge to his cheeks to disguise his facial hair. When Mrs Mills entered the cell she washolding a handkerchief to her face which at the time was normal behaviour for a woman bidding farewell to a friend who was about to be executed. The countess wanted her husband to walk out with his face covered in the same way. The guards, thanks to her buying them a drink a day earlier, allied to their belief that the prisoner would soon be pardoned, were not on full alert. After Mrs Mills left the countess helped her husband dress as a woman and then led him out of the cell past the unsuspecting guards. The couple went straight to a pre-arranged safe house and spent three days there lying low, living on bread and wine. On the Saturday night they sneaked into the residence of the Venetian ambassador where a servant hid the earl in his own room, without the ambassador's knowledge. The following Wednesday the ambassador was taken by coach and horses to Dover to meet his brother who was arriving from the Continent. The earl, dressed in the livery of a servant, joined his retinue. Once there he boarded a small boat which had been hired by Mr Mitchell, the ambassador's young servant who had hidden the earl in the embassy, and set sail for Calais and freedom.

     Alas there was not a happy ending for the couple. The countess eventually joined her husband in France and they lived out their lives in Rome. However, they had left all their assets behind and had to rely on hand-outs by their hosts to survive and they were constantly in debt. The earl died in 1744 and the resourceful Winifred survived him by five years. During that time, honourable till the end, she managed, with great difficulty, to pay off all the debts he had accumulated while in exile.

Chapter five:

Slaves in America

Official figures suggest as many as five million Americans claim Scots descent. However, it's estimated that figure could much higher, with the true number being possibly four times greater. Many of their forebears had arrived in the States during the 17th century. They'd gone to the new world seeking religious freedom and economic opportunities.

But thousands of Scots crossed the Atlantic not as settlers, but as slaves. They were sent there in shackles as a punishment for siding with the king against the forces of the victorious Oliver Cromwell in the English Civil War.

The first Scots slaves were captured after the Battle of Dunbar in September 1650. Cromwell's Parliamentary Army routed the locals who were loyal to King Charles II. Over 3000 Scots were killed and more than 10,000 were taken prisoner.

Half of them were set free because they were seriously wounded and posed no further military threat to the English, who went on to occupy Edinburgh. The rest were force-marched south to Durham. It took a week to get there and nearly half died along the way from their wounds or starvation. The survivors were jailed in Durham Cathedral and were not well cared for by their captors. During the weeks that followed cold, malnutrition and disease led to further loss of life. Over 5000 Scotsmen were taken from Dunbar but less than a third survived and they were transported to the new world as indentured servants. It meant they were forced to work in conditions akin to slavery for up to ten years before being released. Many of them found themselves in New England.

The next mass transportation of Scots slaves took place in the aftermath of the Battle of Worcester. About nine months after the Dunbar massacre Cromwell was still occupying Edinburgh and parts of lowland Scotland. Most of the Scots army still loyal to King Charles II were at Stirling, in an impregnable position. With the Dunbar debacle still fresh in his mind, the Scottish commander, David Leslie, refused to launch another attack. King Charles, however, wanted to invade England, believing his loyal subjects would swell his forces. In July 1651 at Inverkeithing, on the north side of the Forth, the two armies clashed again. There were many casualties on both sides, but the English emerged victorious, again.

Cromwell was a master tactician and after Inverkeithing he appeared to have completely outwitted the Scots yet again. Instead of laying siege to Stirling his army headed north, apparently leaving England defenceless. When the Scots decided to take the bait and invade England he promptly about-turned and began chasing the royalists, who had deserted the safety of Stirling and crossed the Border at Carlisle.

Unfortunately, few Englishmen leapt to his cause, mainly because his Scottish soldiers were regarded as invaders rather than liberators. By the end of August the Scots were cornered at

Worcester, where they fought a last-ditch battle against the Parliamentarians. The date was September 3, 1651, exactly a year on from the Battle of Dunbar. At the end of the conflict the result was much the same, with 4000 royalist fatalities and around 10,000, mostly Scots, in captivity. King Charles managed to escape to exile in France, while David Leslie was sent to the Tower of London for nine years. The prisoners were marched to London and of those who survived many were shipped to the new world as 10-year slaves. Some joined their countrymen in New England while others found themselves in Virginia.

GATHERING OF THE CLANS

CLAN MEMORABILIA FROM LANG SYNE

Books, postcards, Teddy bears, keyrings, mugs and much more...

Visit our website:
www.langsyneshop.co.uk

or write to us:
Lang Syne Publishing,
79 Main Street, Newtongrange,
Midlothian EH22 4NA
Tel: 0131 344 0414
E-mail: info@lang-syne.co.uk